the
**gluten-
free**
cookbook

This edition first published in Great Britain in 2006 by
Kyle Cathie Limited

ISBN 1 85626 633 8
ISBN 13-digit 978 1 85626 633 8

Copyright © 2005 Kyle Cathie Ltd
Photography copyright © 2005 Gus Filgate
Book design © 2005 Kyle Cathie Ltd

Senior Editor: Helen Woodhall
Designer: Geoff Hayes
Typesetter: Mick Hodson
Stylist: Penny Markham
Home Economist: Annie Nichols
Production: Sha Huxtable and Alice Holloway

Colour reproduction by Scanhouse Pty Ltd
Printed and bound in China by C & C Offset Printers

With thanks and acknowlegement to all the recipe writers
whose talents have contributed to the creation of this book.

With special thanks to Linda Bain, Nicola Donovan, Amanda Fries,
Sarah Lee, Kate McBain and Kate Arthur.

First published in Great Britain in 2005 by Kyle Cathie Limited for
Sainsbury's Supermarkets Limited.

**The eggs used in this book are medium sized. All spoon
measurements for dry ingredients are heaped. 1 teaspoon =
5ml, 1 tablespoon = 15ml. Always use either metric or imperial
measurements when following a recipe - never mix the two.**

contents

introduction - gluten-free living

A gluten-free diet doesn't have to mean spending hours preparing complicated or dull food. With a lot of information, and a little imagination, cooking and eating can be a pleasure again, and this book is full of recipes to ensure that you will never be lacking inspiration.

What is coeliac disease?
Simply put, if you have coeliac disease, your body treats gluten as harmful, which leads to inflammation and irritation. The lining of the small intestine becomes damaged and, as many nutrients are absorbed in this way, this can lead to deficiencies in minerals and other nutrients. Coeliac disease affects children and adults, and often runs in families.

Gluten sensitivity can only be managed by avoiding gluten in all forms. This can be

difficult. For many, the only real option is to avoid gluten on a lifelong basis. Family meals need to be adapted, and eating with friends and in restaurants can be hard, so sticking to a totally gluten-free diet needs perseverance and encouragement. Make use of all the help available. For example, a dietician can help you to adapt your diet without missing out on necessary nutrients.

Foods to avoid
Gluten is a protein found in wheat, and similar proteins are found in barley, rye and oats, so the obvious sources of gluten are baked goods containing wheat flour. This includes bread, cakes, pastries, biscuits, puddings and pies made with pastry. Rye is sometimes used in bread, and barley is often used in brewing, which means that beer is off limits. The jury is out on the subject of oats. Some people with coeliac disease may be able to tolerate moderate amounts of oats, but individual reactions differ and there is also the risk that cross-contamination of oats with flour may have occurred during the processing.

Ingredients and products to avoid:
(unless on Coeliac UK's Food List or supermarket own-brand gluten-free list)

Wheat flour and wheat products
Spelt
Barley
Biscuits
Bran
Bread

foods where wheat flour is used as a binder, filler or processing aid. Wheat starch is processed to remove the protein, but it still contains some traces of gluten as it is not possible to remove all protein. Specially manufactured wheat starch, produced to a different specification, is used in gluten-free processed foods. When flour is used as a processing aid, or as part of another compound, it does not have to be declared on the label. If in doubt, check with the manufacturer, or with the Food List of the Coeliac Society.

Bulgar Wheat

Cake

Cereal Filler

Cereal Protein

Couscous

Liquorice

Malt

Modified Wheat Starch

Oats

Pasta

Pastry

Rusk

Rye

Semolina

Soy Sauce

Triticale Wheat

Wheat Breakfast Cereals

Wheat Starch

Wheatgerm

Baked goods are the most obvious source of gluten, but it is also often used in processed

Products which may contain gluten, or may have used flour during the processing:

Chocolate

Mincemeat

Spices

Stock cubes

Breadcrumbs

Crisps

Sausages

Baking powder

Mustard

Creamed coconut

Naturally gluten-free foods

There are many foods and food products that are naturally gluten-free. Meat, fish, eggs, cheese, milk, fruit and vegetables are all in this category. Rice, beans and some cereals are also gluten-free, although cross-contamination may occur during processing. Be careful with any of these foods in their processed forms, however, as wheat products may have been used as a filler or binder.

Gluten in cooking

The chemical structure of gluten in flour gives baked products their distinctive texture and flavour. The most obvious example of this is what happens when bread dough is kneaded. After several minutes you can see the change in texture – the bread becomes more elastic as the strands of gluten in the flour become stretched and drawn out. When the bread is baked the elasticity of the gluten gives a springy texture. This texture is difficult to recreate in gluten-free cooking and baking, but there are alternatives to wheat flour.

Flour substitutes

There are various types of gluten-free flour on the market. All-purpose gluten-free flour is made from a blend of rice flour, potato flour, buckwheat and maize flour. This can simply be subsituted for ordinary flour in whatever recipe you are following. It is not usually possible simply to substitute other flours for wheat flour – which one you choose depends on what you want to use it for as different flours are better at thickening, or adding bulk or texture when baking. Some flours have a distinctive flavour or texture so a combination of flours may work better in terms of both texture and taste.

Buckwheat flour has an earthy, slightly sour flavour. It has a strong taste and its texture is too gluey for baking, but it lends a nutty flavour to the savoury pancakes and pastas in which it is traditionally used.

Rice flour is a bland-tasting, all-purpose flour; it can be either white or brown. Use it to make muffins or bread, although it will give a denser texture than wheat flour. You can also use it as a thickener.

Chickpea flour is also known as gram flour. Use it to make batters or fritters or mix with other flours when baking.

Cornflour is also fairly bland in flavour. Mix it with rice flour to give a smoother texture.

Potato flour is a fine-textured flour made from cooked, dried and ground potatoes. When mixed with other flours in bread making, it produces a moist bread. It is generally used as a thickener.

Soy flour has a fairly strong flavour, so it is best mixed with other flour in small amounts. It adds moistness to baked goods.

Other gluten-free flours are made from grains such as amaranth, quinoa, tapioca or sorghum.

Many non-wheat flours contain higher proportions of fat and protein than wheat flour so need extra care in storage. Store in airtight glass or plastic containers in a cool, dark place or in the refrigerator.

Before using this book

Always seek the advice of a qualified medical practitioner before embarking on any restrictive diet. If you think you may be suffering from gluten sensitivity or coeliac disease it is essential to get a correct diagnosis before going any further. On diagnosis you should ask to be referred to a dietician who will be able to help you to make the necessary changes to your diet.

Some of the recipes in this book use only naturally gluten-free ingredients. Others have been adapted from recipes which normally would use ordinary flour. The baking chapter contains many useful recipes to help you find that delicious taste and texture that can be so elusive in the gluten-free diet and the desserts will give your tastebuds a gluten-free treat. We hope the recipes in this book will help you to rediscover delicious food and set you on your way to healthy, happy gluten-free living.

main meals

leek and potato soup

This vibrant, warming soup makes a satisfying lunch on a chilly day.

40 mins
prep & cook time

serves 4

126 cals
per serving

2g fat
per serving

3 large potatoes, cut into 1cm (½in) cubes
1 leek, sliced into 5mm (¼in) rounds,
 and well rinsed
750ml (1¼ pints) vegetable stock
200ml (⅓ pint) semi-skimmed milk
 or soya milk
salt and freshly ground black pepper

Heat the oil in a saucepan over a medium heat, stir in the vegetables and cook for 2 minutes.

Add the vegetable stock and bring to the boil over a high heat. When it is boiling turn down the heat to low and simmer for 20 minutes.

When the vegetables are cooked take the saucepan off the heat. With a ladle carefully place 3 ladlefuls of the soup in a blender and blend for 10 seconds. Then pour the blended soup into a big bowl.

Repeat the blending until the saucepan is empty. Pour the blended soup back into the saucepan and reheat gently.

Add the milk, salt and pepper and simmer for 2 minutes more.

asparagus quiche

Pastry is possible with gluten-free flour – enjoy this simple light quiche warm or cold with a crisp green salad.

45 mins		176 cals	10g fat
prep & cook time	serves 4	per serving	per serving

100g (3¹/₂oz) gluten-free flour
50g (2oz) butter, cut into small pieces
4-5 tablespoons water
200g (7oz) virtually fat-free fromage frais
2 eggs
100g (3¹/₂oz) asparagus tips, blanched
   and refreshed
15g (¹/₂oz) freshly grated Parmesan cheese
salt and freshly ground black pepper

Preheat the oven to 180°C/350°F/gas mark 4. Grease a 20cm (8cm) loose-bottomed fluted flan tin.

Place the flour in a bowl, then rub in the butter until the mixture resembles fine breadcrumbs.

Add the water and bring together into a soft ball of dough. Wrap in cling film and leave to rest for 30 minutes in the fridge.

On a lightly floured surface, roll out the pastry and use it to line the flan tin. Gently press the pastry into place with your fingers.

In a bowl mix together the fromage frais, eggs and seasoning. Pour into the flan tin, then arrange the asparagus tips. Sprinkle over the Parmesan cheese and cook for 25 minutes or until golden and firm.

COOK'S TIP
To blanch asparagus tips, cook them in boiling water for 2 minutes, then drain and plunge into cold water or run under the cold tap, to stop the cooking process and retain a fresh green colour.

Variation
Replace the asparagus with blanched courgette slices if you prefer.

smoked ham and mushroom risotto

An easy supper that you can adapt to use up any spare veg – the trick is just to keep stirring!

40 mins	serves 4	**432** cals	**14**g fat
prep & cook time	serves 4	per serving	per serving

25g (1oz) butter
1 tablespoon oil
1 onion, finely chopped
250g (8oz) arborio rice
450ml (³/₄ pint) fresh vegetable stock
150ml (¹/₄ pint) dry white wine
175g (6oz) button mushrooms, wiped
  and sliced
1 red pepper, deseeded and finely sliced
125g (4oz) smoked ham, finely sliced
2 tablespoons lemon juice
2 tablespoons single cream
salt and freshly ground black pepper

Variations
Replace the red pepper with blanched asparagus tips, or add a handful of frozen peas or sweetcorn – whatever takes your fancy!

Replace the cream with low-fat crème fraîche for a lower-fat alternative.

Arborio rice's high starch content makes it particularly suitable for risottos. Other risotto rices include Vialone Nano and carnaroli.

Melt the butter and oil in a large frying pan. Gently fry the onion for 2–3 minutes until it starts to soften. Stir in the rice, making sure it is well coated with the butter and oil, and cook for 1 minute.

Add the stock and wine gradually, allowing the rice to soak up each addition before adding more. Continue to stir and add the stock until the rice is cooked. This will take about 20–25 minutes. Add the mushrooms, pepper, ham, lemon juice and cream, and season to taste.

Cook for 1–2 minutes, then serve immediately.

vegetable and tofu stir-fry with soba noodles

This stir-fry is bursting with colour and flavour and will help you on the way to five a day!

30 mins prep & cook time | **serves 4** | **382 cals** per serving | **27g fat** per serving

1/2 head Chinese leaves
100g (3¹/₂oz) shiitake mushrooms
1 bunch red spring onions
100g (3¹/₂oz) baby corn
100g (3¹/₂oz) mangetout
250g (8oz) firm tofu
2 tablespoons rice flour
1 garlic clove
250g (8oz) soba noodles (buckwheat noodles)
2 tablespoons vegetable oil
100g (3¹/₂oz) beansprouts
2 tablespoons shoyu (Japanese soy sauce)
fresh chives to garnish (optional)

Shred the Chinese leaves into 1cm (¹/₂in) ribbons. Wipe and halve the mushrooms. Trim the spring onions and cut into 5cm (2in) lengths.

Trim the baby corn and top and tail the mangetout. Set all the vegetables aside in small piles. Cut the tofu into 2cm (³/₄in) cubes and dust all over with the rice flour. Peel and crush the garlic.

Bring a large saucepan of water to the boil and cook the noodles according to the instructions on the pack, until just tender. Drain well.

Meanwhile, heat the oil in a wok or large frying pan and add the garlic. Fry for a few seconds and then add the mushrooms, spring onions, baby corn and tofu. Stir fry over a high heat for 3 minutes.

Add the Chinese leaves, beansprouts and mangetout, and sprinkle in the shoyu. Continue to stir-fry for a further 2-3 minutes until the vegetables are just tender.

To serve, divide the noodles between 4 warmed serving plates and top with the stir fried vegetables. Garnish with chives if desired.

COOK'S TIP
Ordinary soy sauce can be used instead of shoyu.

Soba noodles are made from buckwheat flour. Check the packet carefully as some manufacturers add wheat flour to soften the slightly sour taste of buckwheat.

beef with broad beans and spinach

A healthy and delicious dish.

1 hr	⚟	**321** cals	**15**g fat
prep & cook time	serves 4-6	per serving	per serving

1 onion, chopped
3 tablespoons oil
2 garlic cloves, crushed
500g (18oz) beef, cubed
2 dried limes
1kg (2¹/₄lb) broad beans
500g (18oz) spinach
salt and freshly ground black pepper

Preheat the oven to 200°C/400°F/gas mark 6.

Fry the onion in oil until golden. Add the garlic and meat and turn to brown it all over. Sprinkle with salt and pepper, add the limes, cover with water and simmer, covered, for 45 minutes. Add more water if necessary. Cut the limes open.

Take the beans out of their pods, add them to the beef and cook for 10 minutes. Wash the spinach thoroughly and remove the stems. Stir in the spinach and cook for a few more minutes, then serve.

nut roast

A classic dish, packed with protein, that's definitely due for a revival.

prep & cook time   serves 4   630 cals per serving   51g fat per serving

300g (10oz) root vegetables, peeled and coarsely grated (eg potato, parsnip, carrot, celeriac)
1 medium onion, very finely chopped
2 tablespoons vegetable oil
200g (7oz) finely ground nuts
75g (3oz) nuts, chopped to the size of a pea
2 free-range eggs, beaten
1/2 teaspoon ground white pepper
1 teaspoon dried thyme
1 teaspoon salt

Preheat the oven to 170°C/325°F/gas mark 3. Line a 1kg (2lb) loaf tin with non-stick baking parchment.

Gently cook the grated vegetables and onion in the oil, in a non-stick pan, for 10–15 minutes or until tender.

Mix the cooked vegetables together with all the other ingredients and press the mixture into the loaf tin.

Bake for approximately 1 hour. Test by inserting a skewer into the nut roast: it should emerge clean. Leave the nut roast to stand in the tin for 10 minutes before turning out onto a serving plate. Slice carefully using a sharp serrated carving knife.

Variations

Other flavouring ideas: experiment by using different nuts, vegetables and herbs. Garlic, chilli, spices, sun-dried tomatoes or olives can also be added to the basic mixture, according to taste. Or layer up the nut roast with your favourite stuffing.

For vegans: If you prefer not to use egg, leave it out, but bear in mind the loaf will not hold together so well. You may prefer to bake it in individual ramekins to avoid having to slice it.

Serve with: gravy, béchamel (white) sauce, parsley sauce or tomato sauce. Mint sauce, cranberry sauce, Cumberland sauce, apple sauce and redcurrant jelly also go well.

COOK'S TIP
Use your favourite nuts, or mixture of nuts, for this recipe. Pine kernels or sunflower seeds are also suitable.

pasta with ham & vegetable sauce

This quick and simple pasta dish makes a great light lunch or supper.

40 mins
prep & cook time

serves 4

600 cals
per serving

11g fat
per serving

2 tablespoons olive oil
2 onions, finely chopped
4 celery sticks, finely chopped
125g (4oz) mushrooms, thinly sliced
1 x 400g (14oz) can chopped tomatoes
150ml (5fl oz) vegetable stock
150ml (5fl oz) dry white wine
1 tablespoon fresh marjoram, chopped finely
50g (2oz) cooked ham, chopped
500g (1lb) gluten-free pasta
salt and freshly ground black pepper
a few sprigs of marjoram to garnish

Heat the oil in a heavy-based saucepan, and gently fry the onion and celery until soft. Add the mushrooms and cook for a further 2 minutes.

Add the tomatoes, stock, wine, marjoram and seasoning. Bring to the boil slowly and simmer gently for 20-30 minutes.

Meanwhile cook the pasta until al dente according to the pack instructions, and drain. Add the ham to the sauce, pour over the pasta, garnish with marjoram and serve immediately.

brazil nut korma

We think you'll love this delicious take on an Indian classic.

prep & cook time	serves 4	per serving	per serving
30 mins		398 cals	36g fat

3 tablespoons vegetable oil

1 medium onion, sliced

1 clove garlic, crushed

1 red chilli, deseeded and finely chopped

2 teaspoons medium hot curry powder

100g (3^{1}/$_{2}$oz) Brazil nut kernels

75g (3oz) creamed coconut made up to 450ml (16fl oz) with water

1 small cauliflower, cut into small florets

125g (4oz) broccoli, cut into small florets

2 courgettes, chopped into small chunks

Heat the oil in a frying pan and fry the onion, garlic, chilli and curry powder for 5 minutes.

Purée half the Brazil nut kernels in a food processor. Add the ground Brazil nuts to the coconut liquid and pour the liquid into the frying pan. Combine and remove from the heat.

Bring a pan of water to the boil and parboil the vegetables: boil the cauliflower for 3 minutes, the broccoli for 2 minutes and the courgette for 1 minute. Drain and refresh in cold water.

Add all the vegetables to the korma sauce and simmer for 4 minutes, stirring in the remaining Brazil nut kernels just before serving.

COOK'S TIP

Experiment with other types of nut in place of the Brazil nuts - cashew nuts make a particularly creamy sauce.

Nutrition: Brazil nuts are quite high in fat, but don't let that put you off them - they are packed with nutrients, especially magnesium and selenium, so the key, of course, is to eat them in moderation.

sea bass with tomato, basil and olive oil crust

Relax and enjoy this delicious gluten-free taste of the Med!

20 mins		281 cals	20g fat
prep & cook time	serves 4	per serving	per serving

4 sun-dried tomatoes
20g (³/₄oz) basil
6 black olives, pitted
25g (1oz) gluten-free breadcrumbs
1 tablespoon olive oil
4 sea bass fillets, scaled, skin on
freshly ground black pepper

Place all the ingredients, except the sea bass, in a food processor and blend to a paste.

Spread this mixture onto the skin side of the fish fillets.

Heat a non-stick pan and fry the bass skin side down for 2-3 minutes. Turn the fish over carefully and cook for a further minute. Serve immediately.

COOK'S TIP
To oven cook the fish, bake in a preheated oven at 180°C/350°F/gas mark 4 for 30-35 minutes.

Serving tip: Serve with shaved fennel and crushed new potatoes.

chicken tandoori

Make your own favourite take-away dish that's great for a night in front of the telly!

1-2 hrs
prep & cook time

serves 4

175 cals
per serving

3g fat
per serving

500g (18oz) boneless, skinless chicken breasts
2 garlic cloves, crushed
150g (5oz) carton natural yogurt
1 tablespoon lemon juice
1 teaspoon grated fresh ginger
large pinch of chilli powder (or cayenne pepper)
1 teaspoon ground coriander
1 teaspoon ground cumin
1/2 teaspoon ground turmeric

Cut the chicken into 3cm (1in) cubes and place in a shallow ovenproof dish. Mix the garlic, yogurt, lemon juice and spices and spread over the chicken.

Cover and marinate in the fridge for at least 1 hour.

Preheat the oven to 200°C/400°F/gas mark 6. Bake the chicken in the marinade for 35 minutes, turning once or twice during cooking.

Alternatively, thread the chicken on to skewers and cook under a preheated hot grill for 15-20 minutes. Chunks of blanched vegetables could be added to the skewers, if you like.

crunchy polenta fish cakes

A real family favourite, these fish cakes make a great lunch or light supper.

prep & cook time	serves 4	367 cals per serving	11g fat per serving

125g (4oz) brown rice
500g (1lb) cod or other firm white fish
2 tablespoons crème fraîche
1 tablespoon fresh coriander, chopped finely
1 tablespoon fresh mint, chopped finely
juice of 1/2 lemon
3 tablespoons polenta
30g (1¼oz) gluten-free plain crisps,
    crunched up fairly small
1 tablespoon olive oil
salt and freshly ground black pepper

Cook the rice in a pan of boiling water for 30-35 minutes or until very soft. Drain and set to one side.

Mash the fish, crème fraîche and rice together, or purée in a food processor, until roughly combined but not smooth.

Stir in the coriander, mint, lemon juice and seasoning. Cover and chill.

Mix the polenta and crisps. Divide the fish mixture into 8 equal-sized portions. Shape each portion into a cake and roll in the polenta and crisp mixture.

Fry the fish cakes in the oil for 5 minutes on each side. Serve piping hot with a leafy green salad.

COOK'S TIP
Replace the polenta and crisps with gluten-free breadcrumbs.

prawn satay

These tasty prawn satay are perfect for summer entertaining or a midweek treat.

25 mins		223 cals	14g fat
prep & cook time	serves 4	per serving	per serving

2 teaspoons sesame oil
1 red chilli, finely chopped
1 clove garlic, crushed
2cm (³/₄in) root ginger, finely grated
¹/₂ teaspoon ground turmeric
25g (1oz) ground almonds
150ml (¹/₄ pint) coconut milk
8 raw king prawns, peeled and cleaned or
    200g (7oz) frozen tiger prawns, defrosted

You will need 4 bamboo or metal skewers.

Heat the oil in a frying pan and fry the chilli, garlic, ginger and turmeric. Add the ground almonds and coconut milk and simmer for 2-3 minutes. Remove from the heat and leave to cool.

Arrange the prawns on the skewers and marinate in the sauce for 5 minutes.

Grill the skewered prawns under a preheated hot grill for 2 minutes each side until cooked through. Heat through the remaining sauce and serve separately.

COOK'S TIP
Soak bamboo skewers in cold water before using, to ensure they don't burn.

thai red prawn curry

This simple curry is quick to make - just the thing for relaxed midweek entertaining.

| prep & cook time | serves 4 | 623 cals per serving | 55g fat per serving |

1 tablespoon pure chilli powder
1 tablespoon ground pure coriander
1 tablespoon finely chopped garlic
1 tablespoon galangal or ground ginger
1 teaspoon salt
1 tablespoon grated lime zest
1 teaspoon freshly ground black pepper
1 small onion, coarsely chopped
1 stalk lemongrass, chopped
4 tablespoons vegetable oil

250g (8oz) block creamed coconut, dissolved
    in 250ml (8fl oz) hot water
1 teaspoon shrimp paste or anchovy paste
500g (1lb) shelled prawns
1 cucumber, cut lengthways, seeded and cut
    into 1cm (1/2in) moons
chopped fresh coriander leaves to garnish
Thai fragrant rice, to serve

Put the first 10 ingredients into a food processor or blender and blend together to form a smooth paste. (You may need to add a little water.)

In a wok or large pan, bring the dissolved coconut cream to the boil. Add the paste you have made and cook over a low heat for 10 minutes, until a film of oil appears around the edge of the pan.

Add the shrimp or anchovy paste, the prawns and the cucumber. Cook gently for 3-4 minutes if the prawns are already cooked, or for 10 minutes if they are raw.

Stir well, garnish with the chopped coriander and serve immediately with Thai fragrant rice.

Check labels carefully: some ingredients such as shrimp paste or creamed coconut have wheat-related products in the ingredients list.

black-eyed bean casserole with lime and coriander

A healthy vegetarian style dish with a delicious mix of herbs and spices.

1-2 hrs		268 cals	11g fat
prep & cook time	serves 4-6	per serving	per serving

For the casserole:
250g (9oz) black-eyed beans
2 tablespoons sunflower oil
1 onion, finely chopped
2 garlic cloves, finely chopped
1 tablespoon paprika
1 birds eye chilli, deseeded and finely chopped
125g (4¹/₂oz) carrots, peeled and cut into
  1cm (¹/₂in) dice
400g (14oz) can chopped tomatoes
326g can sweetcorn
dash of tabasco
¹/₂ x 15g pack fresh coriander, finely chopped
salt and freshly ground black pepper

For the lime and coriander cream: (optional)
125ml (4fl oz) soured cream
¹/₂ x 15g pack fresh coriander, roughly chopped
1 tablespoon lime juice

To make the casserole, soak the black-eyed beans in water overnight, drain and boil in plenty of water until tender, approximately 45 minutes.

Heat the oil in a pan and cook the onion until golden brown. Add the garlic just as the onions are browning.

Add the paprika, chilli and carrots and cook slowly until the carrots are 'al dente'. The mixture in the pan will resemble a thick paste.

Pour in the can of tomatoes and drained black-eyed beans and simmer gently for 5 minutes.

Add the sweetcorn, a dash of tabasco and seasoning, continue to simmer for 6-7 minutes making sure that it does not dry out. Remove from the heat and sprinkle over the coriander.

For the lime and coriander cream, mix together the soured cream, coriander and lime juice. Season to taste before serving with the casserole.

lamb and lime leaf burgers with peanut sauce

Everyone's favourite - with an exotic twist.

prep & cook time | serves 8 | 1000 cals per serving | 60g fat per serving

2 eggs
2 tablespoons *nam pla* (Thai fish sauce)
15 lime leaves
2kg (4¹/₂lb) finely minced lamb
150g (5oz) cornflour
1 teaspoon salt
2 cloves garlic, peeled and finely chopped
1 medium red onion, peeled and finely chopped

For the peanut sauce:
1 tablespoon oil
12 mild red chillies, finely chopped
50g (2oz) red Thai shallots, peeled and
   finely chopped
1 garlic clove, crushed
1 small knob ginger, peeled and finely grated
4 lime leaves
300ml (¹/₂ pint) coconut milk
200ml (7fl oz) crunchy peanut butter
2 tablespoons tamarind paste
50g (2oz) grated palm sugar
1 tablespoon *nam pla* (Thai fish sauce)

Put into a blender the eggs, fish sauce and lime leaves and blend for 20 seconds. Scrape down the bowl then blend again for a further 20 seconds. Sieve the mixture to remove fibres and stems.

Place the minced lamb In a mixing bowl with the cornflour, salt, garlic, onion and lime paste. Mix well.

Shape the mix into burgers approximately 1cm (¹/₂in) thick. Place in the fridge for up to 2 days, until needed.

For the peanut sauce, heat the oil in the pan. Add the chilli, shallots, garlic, ginger and lime leaves and cook until softened.

Add the coconut milk, peanut butter, tamarind paste and grated palm sugar. Bring to a simmer, stirring well, then check the seasoning and add fish sauce to taste.

Cook the burgers on a skillet or in a frying pan and serve with a dollop of peanut sauce and a leafy green salad.

COOK'S TIPS
The lime leaf mixture is a fairly small quantity, so if you have a herb blender or spice grinder use that instead of a full-size blender.

Palm sugar is made from the sap of the coconut palm. Dark demerara sugar can be substituted but will not give exactly the same effect.

Tamarind paste, made from the pods of the tamarind tree, is often used in south-east Asian cookery. It has a pungent lemony flavour.

roasted vegetable pizza

A family favourite, bursting with nutritious and delicious vegetables.

2½ hrs prep & cook time

serves 4

558 cals per serving

30g fat per serving

250g (8oz) gluten-free flour
½ teaspoon salt
15g (½oz) fresh yeast
1 egg
lukewarm water
1 small aubergine, cut into wedges
1 red, green and yellow pepper, deseeded and
  cut into sixths
1 courgette, sliced into 1cm (½in) pieces
25g (1oz) mushrooms, wiped and halved
3 cloves garlic, cut into half lengthways
1 tablespoon fresh rosemary, coarsely chopped
3 tablespoons olive oil
1 tablespoon sun-dried tomato paste
1 tablespoon fresh basil leaves
40g (1½oz) sun-dried tomatoes, chopped
75g (3oz) Gruyère cheese, grated
freshly ground black pepper

Preheat the oven to 200°C/400° F/gas mark 6.
You will need a 28cm (11in) pizza tin or
baking tray.

Sieve the flour and salt into a bowl and crumble
in the yeast. Beat the egg with a little water. Add
to the flour mixture to make a stiff dough,
adding a little more water if necessary.

Leave the dough in a warm place to rise.

Meanwhile, roast the vegetables and garlic
cloves on a baking tray, sprinkled with the
rosemary and olive oil, for 25-30 minutes until
softened.

Roll out the dough, place in the tin or on a
baking sheet and spread over the sun-dried
tomato paste. Arrange the roasted vegetables on
top. Sprinkle with the basil leaves and sun-dried
tomatoes, cover with the Gruyère cheese and
bake for 25 minutes until the base is crispy and
the cheese melted.

**Note: If you haven't got time to make your
own pizza base, you can buy gluten-free
pizza bases.**

easy three-cheese and rocket pizza

Quick and easy to prepare, this cheat's pizza makes a great weekday supper.

 25 mins
prep & cook time

 serves 1

 691 cals
per serving

 18g fat
per serving

1 gluten-free pizza base
75g (3oz) tomato and herb pizza topping
20g (³/₄oz) Cheddar cheese, grated
20g (³/₄oz) freshly grated mozzarella
1 tablespoon mascarpone
7 pitted black olives
1 handful rocket leaves
salt and freshly ground black pepper

Preheat the oven to 220°C/425°F/gas mark 7.

Place the pizza base on a baking tray, then spread over the pizza topping to within 5mm (¹/₄in) of the edge. Sprinkle over the Cheddar and mozzarella and finish with the mascarpone.

Scatter over the olives and season to taste. Place the pizza directly onto the top oven shelf, placing a baking tray on the shelf below, and cook for 10 minutes or until golden brown and crisp.

Remove from the oven and top with the rocket leaves. Serve immediately.

Note: If you can't find gluten-free pizza bases, follow the recipe on the previous page to make your own.

beef casserole and dumplings

A delicious winter warmer you'll come back to throughout
the year.

prep & cook   serves 6   per   per
time   serving   serving

1kg (2lb) braising beef
2 tablespoons cornflour
2 tablespoons vegetable oil
25g (1oz) butter or margarine
1 large onion, sliced
125g (4oz) unsmoked streaky bacon,
   cut into strips
1 large carrot, cut into large dice
2 sticks celery, cut into large dice
12 sage leaves, finely chopped
1 sprig rosemary, finely chopped
3 garlic cloves, crushed
1 bottle full-bodied red wine
250g (8oz) chestnut mushrooms
salt and freshly ground black pepper

For the dumplings:
50g (2oz) buckwheat flour
50g (2oz) rice flour
75g (3oz) potato flour
2 heaped teaspoons baking powder
20g (³/₄oz) flat-leaf parsley
75g (3oz) lard, frozen and grated
salt and freshly ground black pepper

Preheat oven to 150°C/300°F/gas mark 2

Coat the beef in the cornflour and fry it in the oil
and butter in a roomy casserole until lightly
browned. Add the onion and bacon and fry for a
further couple of minutes.

Stir in the carrot, celery, sage, rosemary, garlic,
salt and freshly ground black pepper. Add the
red wine and cover with a tight fitting lid.
Transfer to the oven and simmer for 2¹/₂ hours.
Add the mushrooms and return to the oven for a
further 20 minutes.

To make the dumplings. Mix all the flours and
baking powder, seasoning and parsley in a bowl.
Blend in the lard and add enough cold water to
form a dough. Shape into 12 dumplings.

Add these to the casserole and return to the
oven for about 30 minutes or until the
dumplings are light and fluffy. Serve piping hot.

COOK'S TIP
**Lard replaces traditional suet in these
dumplings because most suet is coated
with flour.**

side dishes

avocado and tomato salsa

Serve this salsa as a dip with tortilla chips, or as a side dish with grilled fish or meat.

15 mins	**serves 4**	**100** cals	**5**g fat
prep time	serves 4	per serving	per serving

2 large ripe tomatoes
2 spring onions, trimmed
1 small red onion, peeled
1/2 ripe avocado
1 fresh red and green chilli
juice of 1 lime or lemon
2 teaspoons freshly chopped parsley
2 teaspoons freshly chopped coriander
sea salt and freshly ground black pepper

Skin and seed the tomatoes, then cut the flesh into tiny dice. Finely dice the spring onions. Dice the red onion and avocado, then seed and dice the chillies. Gently fold all these together with the lemon or lime juice, parsley and coriander. Season with salt and pepper.

Chill until required.

Note: Vary the amount of chilli to suit your taste.

chorizo, feta and beetroot salad

We love this brilliant combination of flavours and colours - great as a side dish or a light lunch.

prep time   serves 4   per serving   per serving

For the dressing:
1 tablespoon olive oil
1 tablespoon wholegrain mustard
6 tablespoons balsamic vinegar
dash of tabasco sauce
1 teaspoon caraway seeds, pounded with a
  little olive oil

750g (1¹/₂lb) cooked beetroot, cut into
  wedges
20g (³/₄oz) fresh flat-leaf parsley or
  coriander
2 small red onions, diced very small
150g (5oz) chorizo sausages, sliced and fried
mixed salad leaves, to serve
75g (3oz) feta cheese, crumbled
coarse sea salt and freshly ground black
  pepper

Mix the oil, mustard, vinegar, tabasco and caraway seeds to make a thin dressing.

Pour over the beetroot wedges and leave for half an hour in a cool place, for the flavours to develop.

Before serving, mix in the parsley or coriander, red onion, seasoning and chorizo.

Arrange the mixed salad leaves on a large plate or serving dish and arrange the beetroot and sausage mixture on top, followed by the crumbled feta cheese.

COOK'S TIP
Replace the chorizo with walnuts for a vegetarian alternative.

Check that your mustard and chorizos are gluten-free - some brands may contain wheat products.

fresh corn pakora

Great as a starter or as a side dish with your favourite meat or fish dishes.

45 mins — prep & cook time

serves 4

382 cals — per serving

27g fat — per serving

6 sweetcorn cobs
1-3 tablespoons gram flour
1 teaspoon sugar
¼ teaspoon ground turmeric
2 tablespoons natural yogurt
1 tablespoon chopped fresh coriander
4 fresh green chillies, de-seeded and chopped
1cm (½in) piece fresh ginger, peeled and grated
vegetable oil for frying
salt

Grate the sweetcorn directly from the cobs into a sieve and leave to drain.

Meanwhile, put 1 heaped tablespoon of gram flour and all the other ingredients, except the oil, in a bowl and season with salt.

Add the corn and mix well. If the mixture is too wet, add another 1-2 spoonfuls of flour.

Pour oil to a depth of about 5cm (2in) into a deep-fryer or large saucepan and heat until hot enough to brown a cube of bread in 30 seconds. The oil should be at a temperature of approximately 190°C/375°F.

Shape the corn mixture into small balls and fry in batches in the hot oil over a medium heat for 5-6 minutes until light brown. Drain on absorbent paper and serve hot.

COOK'S TIP
If sweetcorn isn't in season, replace the sweetcorn cobs with 200g (7oz) frozen or tinned sweetcorn. Chop roughly before proceeding with the recipe.

Gram flour, also known as besan, is made from chickpeas. It is commonly used to make biscuits, bhajis, pakoras and fritters.

deep-fried cheddar balls

These crunchy treats are perfect served with pre-dinner drinks or passed around at a buffet or barbecue.

30 mins		**85** cals	**6**g fat
prep & cook time	serves 16-18	per serving	per serving

250g (8oz) Cheddar cheese, grated finely
2 large eggs, beaten
2 tablespoons gram flour
$1/4$ teaspoon baking powder
1 fresh green chilli, de-seeded and chopped
2-3 teaspoons chopped fresh coriander
$1/4$ teaspoon salt
vegetable oil for frying
tomato chutney to serve

Put the cheese, eggs, flour, baking powder, chilli, coriander and salt in a bowl and mix together thoroughly. If the mixture is too wet, add a little more flour; if it is too dry, mix in a little more beaten egg white.

Pour oil to a depth of about 5cm (2in) into a deep-fryer or large saucepan and heat until hot enough to brown a cube of bread in 30 seconds.

Meanwhile, shape teaspoons of the cheese mixture into small balls. Carefully transfer the cheese balls to the hot oil and cook in batches for 2-3 minutes, until golden.

Drain on kitchen paper, then serve hot, skewered on cocktail sticks, accompanied by tomato chutney.

wild rice & apricot salad

This fresh fruity salad is perfect for summer barbecues or outdoor feasts.

40 mins		257 cals	7g fat
prep & cook time	serves 4-6	per serving	per serving

75g (3oz) long grain rice
75g (3oz) wild rice
125g (4oz) dried apricots
50g (2oz) blanched almonds
150g (5oz) natural yogurt
75g (3oz) raisins
2 tablespoons finely chopped parsley
salt and freshly ground black pepper

Preheat the oven to 200°C/400°F/gas mark 6.

Cook the rice according to instructions. Rinse and refresh in cold water.

Roughly chop the dried apricots. Place the almonds on a baking tray and roast in the preheated oven for 2-3 minutes until golden brown.

When the nuts are cool, mix all the ingredients together and season to taste.

If you prefer, dry-fry the almonds in a non-stick pan for several minutes, shaking frequently to prevent burning.

vegetables in piquant sauce

Hot as a side dish or cold as a salad - either way this sweet and sour dish tastes delicious.

35 mins		**115** cals	**7**g fat
prep & cook time	serves 4-6	per serving	per serving

For the paste:

2 shallots or 1/2 onion, chopped

2 garlic cloves, chopped

3 candlenuts or 5 blanched almonds, chopped

1 large red or green chilli, deseeded and chopped

1/2 teaspoon ground turmeric

2 tablespoons white wine vinegar

2 tablespoons groundnut or olive oil

1/2 teaspoon salt

125ml (4fl oz) water

8-10 small pickling onions, peeled (optional)

175g (6oz) French beans, topped and tailed and cut into 2 or 3 pieces

175g (6oz) carrots, peeled and cut into sticks about the same length as the beans

175g (6oz) cauliflower florets

8-10 small red or green chillies (optional)

1 teaspoon mustard powder

1 teaspoon sugar

1 tablespoon white distilled vinegar

salt and freshly ground black pepper to taste

Put all the ingredients for the paste in a blender or food processor and blend until smooth.

Transfer this paste to a wok or a large shallow saucepan. Bring to the boil, stirring most of the time, for 4 minutes.

Add the water and bring back to the boil. When it is boiling, add the pickling onions (if used), stir, and cover the wok or pan for 2 minutes.

Uncover and add the beans and carrots, put the cover on again and simmer for 3 minutes.

Once more uncover the wok or pan, and add the cauliflower and the rest of the ingredients. Stir and cover. Continue cooking for 3-5 minutes.

Uncover the wok or pan for the last time, adjust the seasoning and turn the vegetables over again for a few seconds.

Transfer to a warm serving dish, if it is to be served hot as an accompaniment to your main course; otherwise chill, to be served cold a few hours or days later.

Candlenuts are small, white, waxy nuts similar in shape to hazelnuts. They can sometimes be found in Asian or Indian shops. Almonds, macadamias or Brazil nuts can be substituted.

baked courgettes, feta and tomatoes

A colourful mediterranean style starter or side dish!

30 mins		**164 cals**	**13g fat**
prep & cook time	serves 4	per serving	per serving

1 pack yellow courgettes, cut in half
  lengthways
2 tablespoons olive oil
3 tomatoes, halved
1 tablespoon balsamic vinegar
½ x 200g (7oz) pack feta, diced
few sprigs lemon thyme, picked
15g pack basil leaves for garnishing (optional)
salt and freshly ground black pepper

Preheat the oven to 200°C/400°F/gas mark 6.

Heat a griddle pan. Brush the courgettes with
olive oil and cook them quickly for 2 minutes on
the flesh side until lightly charred.

Repeat the process with the tomatoes.

Put the courgettes and tomatoes into a shallow
ovenproof dish and season. Drizzle over the
balsamic vinegar, the remaining olive oil, diced
feta, lemon thyme and seasoning.

Cook in the oven for 20-30 minutes or until the
courgettes are tender.

Serve with some fresh basil leaves.

bacon and chestnut sprouts

Too good to save for Christmas Day, you'll be enjoying these sprouts all winter.

 30 mins
prep & cook time

 serves 4

 280 cals
per serving

 17g fat
per serving

375g (12oz) Brussels sprouts, trimmed
25g (1oz) butter
4 rashers smoked streaky bacon, chopped
200g (7oz) cooked and peeled chestnuts, halved
salt and freshly ground black pepper

Place the Brussels sprouts in a large pan of boiling water and cook for 5-8 minutes until just tender.

Melt the butter in a large frying pan and add the bacon. Fry until crispy.

Add the chestnuts and drained sprouts and cook for a further minute, mixing well. Season to taste and serve hot.

peela aloo - yellow spiced potatoes

Throw out the masher and enjoy these great spicy potatoes instead!

35 mins		367 cals	21g fat
prep & cook time	serves 4-6	per serving	per serving

6-8 medium potatoes, peeled
125ml (4fl oz) vegetable oil
2 garlic cloves, chopped
1 teaspoon ground turmeric
1 teaspoon salt
1/2 teaspoon chilli powder
1/2 teaspoon ground cumin
1/2 teaspoon mustard seeds

Cook the whole potatoes in boiling water for 25-30 minutes, until just cooked through. Do not overcook. Drain and leave to cool, then cut into bite-sized pieces and put in a large saucepan.

Heat the oil in a small frying pan and cook the garlic, turmeric, salt, chilli powder, cumin and mustard seeds for 3-4 minutes, until the garlic has browned.

Pour the spice mixture over the potatoes, mix well and cook over a medium heat for a few minutes, until quite hot. Serve immediately.

baking

blueberry muffins

These tasty muffins, bursting with vitamin-packed berries, are great for breakfast or an afternoon treat.

35 mins		198 cals	8g fat
prep & cook time	makes 12	per serving	per serving

50g (2oz) margarine
150g (5oz) caster sugar
2 eggs
200g (7oz) rice flour
1 teaspoon baking powder
175ml (6fl oz) sour cream
150g (5oz) blueberries
1/2 teaspoon vanilla essence

Preheat the oven to 220°C/425°F/gas mark 7.

Cream the margarine and sugar together until light and fluffy. Add the eggs and combine.

Sieve the flour and baking powder together and add to the egg mixture with the sour cream.

Stir in the blueberries and vanilla essence.

Divide the mixture between 12 large muffin cases, and bake for 15-20 minutes until golden and risen.

Variation:
Replace the blueberries with cranberries or sultanas.

cheese scones

These savoury scones are great served for lunch with a hearty bowl of soup.

prep & cook time	makes 10-12	per serving	per serving
30 mins		**177** cals	**6g** fat

1 egg
250ml (8fl oz) milk
375g (12oz) all-purpose gluten-free flour
5 teaspoons baking powder
125g (4oz) Cheddar cheese, grated
1 tablespoon Parmesan cheese, grated
salt and cayenne pepper

Preheat the oven to 220°C/425°F/gas mark 7.

Beat the egg and milk together.

Sieve the flour and baking powder together, stir in most of the grated Cheddar and Parmesan, reserving about 2 tablespoons, and season with the salt and cayenne pepper.

Make a well in the centre and pour in the egg and milk. Mix until combined but be careful not to overwork the mixture.

Roll out the scone mix until it is about 2.5cm (1in) thick, and use a 6cm (2½in) cutter to cut out the scones. Sprinkle with the remaining grated cheese.

Bake for 15-20 minutes until golden and cooked through.

COOK'S TIP
Use your imagination to add variety to your scones: add thyme leaves, rosemary or chopped chillis. Or try olives, sun-dried tomatoes or sultanas – whatever you like.

chocolate brownies

Everybody's favourite - the classic chocolate treats.

50 mins — prep & cook time

makes 16-20

211 cals — per serving

14g fat — per serving

125g (4oz) butter
200g (7oz) soft brown sugar
125g (4oz plain chocolate, chopped
50g (2oz) rice flour
20g (³/₄oz) cocoa powder
¹/₄ teaspoon baking powder
3 eggs
150g (5oz) nuts, such as almonds, walnuts or
    hazelnuts, or a mixture.

Preheat the oven to 180°C/350°F/gas mark 4. Grease and line a 20 x 20cm (8 x 8in) baking tin.

Place the butter, sugar and chocolate in a bowl over a pan of simmering water and stir until melted.

Sift the flour, cocoa powder and baking powder into the mix and stir well. Add the eggs and nuts.

Pour into the baking tin and bake for 35 minutes until cooked through but still quite soft in the centre.

Cut into slices and cool on a wire rack.

gingerbread men

Great for kids young and old - dress your gingerbread
men to impress.

prep & cook   makes   per   per
time   12   serving   serving

275g (9oz) gluten-free plain flour
1¹/₂ teaspoons ground pure ginger
¹/₂ teaspoon bicarbonate of soda
125g (4oz) butter
125g (4oz) caster sugar
2 tablespoons golden syrup, melted

Preheat oven to 170°C/325°F/gas mark 3.

Sieve the flour, ginger and bicarbonate of soda
into a large bowl. Rub in the butter.

Stir in the sugar, then add the syrup and mix to a
dough, adding a little water if the dough is too
dry and a little more flour if too sticky.

Roll out between two sheets of greaseproof
paper to approximately 5mm (¹/₄in) thick.
Cut out the gingerbread men with a 10cm
(4in) cutter.

Place carefully on a greased baking tray and
bake for 10 minutes. Leave to cool slightly then
transfer to a wire rack.

Decorate with icing and sweets as desired.

COOK'S TIP
Replace the butter with dairy-free spread if
you are cooking for a vegan or someone who
is avoiding dairy produce.

Make sure that the sweets you use for
decoration are also gluten-free. Check with
the manufacturer if in any doubt.

crumble-topped mince pies

A tastily topped pie that's set to become a year-round treat.

| prep & cook time | makes 10 | 382 cals per serving | 27g fat per serving |

175g (6oz) butter or dairy-free margarine
375g (12oz) gluten-free flour
50g (2oz) ground almonds
25g (1oz) caster sugar
375g (12oz) gluten-free mincemeat

Preheat the oven to 200°C/400°F/gas mark 6.

Place the butter or margarine in a bowl with the flour. Rub together until they resemble fine breadcrumbs. Stir in the ground almonds.

Set aside 100g (3¹/₂oz) of the mixture and stir the sugar into it. Bind the remaining mixture together with 3-4 tablespoons of cold water and bring together to form a firm dough.

Divide the pastry dough into 10 equal portions and press into 10 lightly greased muffin tins. Neaten the edges and chill for 30 minutes.

Divide the mincemeat between the pastry cases and sprinkle each with the reserved crumble mixture.

Bake in the oven for 20 minutes, until lightly golden. Leave to cool for 20 minutes before removing from the tin. Serve warm or cold.

chocolate biscuit slice

No baking involved but can you wait the hour this sweet treat takes to set?

1½ hr prep & cook time

makes 24

158 cals per serving

11g fat per serving

150g (5oz) unsalted butter
150g (5oz) plain chocolate, broken into pieces
2 tablespoons golden syrup
6 cardamom pods, seeds removed and crushed
200g (7oz) packet gluten-free chocolate
    biscuits, roughly crushed
75g (3oz) cashew nuts, roughly chopped
6 glacé cherries, washed and quartered
75g (3oz) apricots, cut into strips
40g (1½oz) marzipan bar, cut into 1cm
    (½in) cubes

Line a 12 x 30cm (5 x 12in) shallow dish with cling film, leaving an overhang.

Place the butter, chocolate and syrup in a heatproof bowl over a saucepan of boiling water and stir occasionally until melted.

Remove from the heat and allow to cool slightly, then stir in the crushed cardamom seeds. Place the biscuits, cashew nuts, cherries, apricots and marzipan bar in a large mixing bowl and pour over the chocolate mixture, stirring well to combine.

Pour the mixture into the prepared dish, press down with a metal spoon, then smooth over the top.

Cover with the overhanging cling film and refrigerate for at least an hour. Turn out on to a clean board, remove the cling film and cut into 24 pieces.

COOK'S TIP
Choose unsulphured dried apricots where possible. They don't have the same orange appearance as treated dried apricots but do contain fewer additives.

banana bread

This lower-fat bread is a guilt-free indulgence!

2 hr
prep & cook time

serves 12

143 cals
per serving

3g fat
per serving

125g (4oz) butter
125g (4oz) caster sugar
2 eggs
3 large ripe bananas, mashed
175g (6oz) ground rice flour
50g (2oz) cornflour
1 teaspoon mixed spice
2 teaspoons baking powder
¼ teaspoon salt

Preheat the oven to 180°C/350°F/gas mark 4.
Grease and line a 1kg (2lb) loaf tin.

Cream the butter and sugar until light and fluffy.
Gradually beat in the eggs, one at a time.

Gently stir in the mashed banana. Sieve the
flours, mixed spice, baking powder and salt into
the mixture and fold until incorporated.

Pour into the loaf tin and bake for 1–1½ hours
until a skewer inserted into the centre of the loaf
comes out clean. Cool on a wire rack.

coconut macaroons

A classic treat for special occasions.

35 mins		**192** cals	**12**g fat
prep & cook time	makes 24	per serving	per serving

25g (1oz) butter
125g (4oz) desiccated coconut
125g (4oz) caster sugar
2 drops vanilla essence
2 egg whites

Preheat the oven to 200°C/400°F/gas mark 6. Cover a baking sheet with baking parchment.

Melt the butter in a saucepan. Mix all the remaining ingredients together with the butter and stir well for 4 minutes.

Shape the mixture into 24 balls and place on the baking parchment.

Place the baking sheet on the middle shelf of the oven and bake for 12 minutes or until golden brown. Remove from the oven and leave to cool on the baking sheet for 15 minutes.

To remove the macaroons, gently slide a butter knife under the macaroons to separate them from the baking parchment.

orange and almond macaroons

The perfect bite for a mid-morning snack.

1 hr		70 cals	3g fat
prep & cook time	makes 18	per serving	per serving

200g (7oz) caster sugar
25g (1oz) granulated sugar
100g (3¹/₂oz) ground almonds
15g (¹/₂oz) ground rice
1 egg white
grated zest of 1 small orange
36 flaked almonds

Preheat the oven to 180°C/350°F/gas mark 4. Line a baking tray with baking parchment or rice paper.

Sift the sugars, almonds and ground rice into a bowl.

Add the egg white and orange zest, and beat thoroughly with an electric beater for 5 minutes.

Allow the mixture to stand for 10 minutes, then continue beating for a further 5 minutes. If the mixture is very wet, add a litle more ground rice until it reaches a piping consistency.

Pile the mixture into a piping bag fitted with a 2.5cm (1in) plain piping nozzle.

Pipe the mixture onto the baking tray. Press a couple of flaked almonds onto the top of each macaroon.

Place in the preheated oven and cook for 20-25 minutes until the macaroons are a light golden brown.

Variation:
Top with gluten-free glacé cherries or walnut halves if you prefer.

COOK'S TIP
These macaroons are also dairy-free.

mixed spice sponge

Serve this gooey cake warm for pudding or cold with cream as a tea-time treat.

prep & cook time

serves 8-10

per serving

per serving

4 eggs, separated
2 tablespoons cornflour
150g (5oz) sugar
25g (1oz) arrowroot
1 teaspoon mixed spice
1 teaspoon ground cinnamon
1 teaspoon ground ginger
1/2 teaspoon cream of tartar
1/2 teaspoon bicarbonate of soda
1 tablespoon golden syrup, warmed

Preheat the oven to 180°C/350°F/gas mark 4. Grease and line a 20cm (8in) cake tin.

Whisk the egg whites until stiff.

Beat the remaining ingredients together and carefully fold into the egg whites.

Pour into the cake tin and bake for 30-35 minutes until golden and firm to the touch. Leave to cool for a few minutes in the tin, then serve warm, or leave to cool on a wire rack.

tofu and orange cake

This deliciously moist flour-free cake tastes just as good as the 'real thing'.

prep & cook time	serves 6-8	507 cals per serving	33g fat per serving

150g (5oz) tofu, drained
200g (7oz) whole brazil nuts
100g (3¹/₂oz) whole almonds
zest of 2 oranges
325g (11oz) fresh pineapple, peeled and
   chopped
40g (1¹/₂oz) fresh ginger, finely chopped
250g (8oz) caster sugar
6 eggs
1¹/₂ teaspoons baking powder

Preheat oven to 180°C/350°F/gas mark 4.

Line a 20cm (8in) spring-form cake tin with baking parchment.

Grate the drained tofu into a large bowl.

Put the brazil nuts and almonds in a food processor and blitz on high speed for 20 seconds or until they resemble fine crumbs. Add the orange zest and blitz again for 5 seconds. Mix with the tofu and combine.

Place the pineapple, ginger and caster sugar in the food processor (no need to wash it after processing the nuts) and blitz for 20 seconds until you have a purée. Add the eggs and baking powder, blitz again for 5 seconds and fold into the nut and tofu mixture.

Pour the mixture into the cake tin and cook for approximately 1 hour and 20 minutes. Test by inserting a skewer into the centre of the cake: if it comes out clean the cake is ready. Place on a baking rack to cool. Dust the cake with a little icing sugar before serving.

COOK'S TIP
Don't expect this cake to rise too much – it has a moist texture, instead of the dry springy texture of a traditional cake.

Serving tip:
The best thing to serve with this is something sour like Greek yogurt, fromage frais or crème fraîche. Tart berries like blackcurrants or gooseberries are fantastic on the side, as are segmented oranges drizzled with a little Cointreau.

ginger cake

This rich and luxurious cake is a real winter warmer.

| prep & cook time | serves 10 | per serving | per serving |

150g (5oz) butter
150g (5oz) muscovado sugar
2 eggs, beaten
4 tablespoons black treacle
2 teabags
150ml (1/2 pint) boiling water
100g (3 1/2oz) raisins
125g (4oz) rice flour
125g (4oz) gluten-free flour
2 level teaspoons baking powder
2 teaspoons ground ginger

Preheat the oven to 170°C/325°F/gas mark 3.

Grease and line a 20cm (8in) cake tin.

Cream the butter with the sugar until light and fluffy. Add the beaten eggs a little at a time until well incorporated.

Stir in the treacle. Place the tea bags in a jug with the boiling water and raisins and leave to soak for 5 minutes.

Sieve the flours, baking powder and ginger into the butter and sugar mixture and fold in carefully with a metal spoon.

Drain the raisins, reserving the liquid, and gently incorporate the raisins and enough liquid to make a cake-like consistency into the mixture. Spoon into the cake tin and smooth the surface with a wet spoon. Bake in the oven for 1 hour or until an inserted skewer comes out clean. Leave to cool in the tin for a few minutes then turn out onto a wire rack to cool.

COOK'S TIP
Replace the butter with dairy-free spread for those who have to avoid dairy products.

fruit cake

A cake you boil? You'd better believe it!

prep & cook time	makes 16-20 slices	per serving	per serving
2 hrs		135 cals	5g fat

100g (3¹/₂oz) butter or margarine
100g (3¹/₂oz) granulated sugar
200g (7oz) mixed dried fruit
150ml (¹/₄ pint) hot water
100g (3¹/₂oz) carrots, grated
2 eggs, beaten
200g (7oz) rice flour
¹/₂ teaspoon bicarbonate of soda
1 teaspoon mixed spice
¹/₄ teaspoon cream of tartar

Preheat the oven to 180°C/350°F/gas mark 4. Grease and line a 20cm (8in) round cake tin.

Put the butter, sugar, dried fruit and water into a large saucepan and bring to the boil.

Simmer for 15 minutes, then remove from the heat and leave to cool.

Mix the carrots with the eggs and stir into the cooled mixture.

Sift together the remaining ingredients and fold into the fruit mixture.

Pour into the prepared cake tin and bake for 50-60 minutes or until a skewer inserted into the centre of the cake comes out clean. Turn out onto a wire rack to cool.

the gluten-free cookbook **97**

christmas cake

A festive treat that everyone can enjoy, this impressive cake will be a real crowd-pleaser.

| prep & cook time | serves 12 | per serving | per serving |

2½ hrs   **serves 12**   **544 cals**   **19g fat**

250g (8oz) butter or margarine
175g (6oz) dark brown sugar
2 tablespoons treacle
2 tablespoons brandy
4 eggs
75g (3oz) cornflour
100g (3½oz) potato flour
1 tablespoon mixed spice
2 teaspoons baking powder
175g (6oz) ground almonds
1kg (2lb) luxury dried fruit mix
finely grated zest of 1 orange

Preheat the oven to 170°C/325°F/gas mark 3.

First prepare the tin. Grease the base and sides of a deep 20cm (8in) cake tin. Cut a double thickness strip of baking parchment 5cm (2in) deeper than the tin and long enough to wrap around the tin completely. Make a 2cm (³/₄in) crease along the long folded edge, then snip the paper from the fold to the crease at regular intervals. Press one paper strip into the tin, grease and then press the other strip on top, making sure the paper folds are flat on the bottom of the tin. Cut 3 rounds of paper to fit the bottom of the tin and press into the base.

In a large mixing bowl, cream together the butter or margarine, sugar and treacle until pale and creamy. Whisk in the brandy and gradually add the eggs and the cornflour, mixing to combine.

Sieve in the potato flour, mixed spice and baking powder, and fold in using a large metal spoon, along with the remaining ingredients.

Pile into the prepared tin and smooth over the top.

Bake in the oven for 2 hours or until a metal skewer inserted into the centre comes out clean, covering the top with foil if it browns too quickly. Leave to cool in the tin (it may sink slightly).

COOK'S TIPS
This cake will keep just like any other fruit cake, and the flavour develops further after 2 days. Before decorating or icing, turn the cake upside down. If you are using bought marzipan and/or icing, check that they are gluten-free.

If you have a nut allergy you can replace the ground almonds with 75g (3oz) more cornflour and 75g (3oz) more potato flour.

seeded bread

The aroma of this bread baking is sure to get your taste buds tingling.

45 mins		283 cals	7g fat
prep & cook time	serves 8	per serving	per serving

150g (5oz) rice flour
150g (5oz) potato flour
150g (5oz) chickpea flour
50g (2oz) millet grain
50g (2oz) pumpkin seeds
50g (2oz) sunflower seeds
15g (½oz) salt
3 teaspoons baking powder
250ml (8fl oz) water

Preheat the oven to 200°C/400°F/gas mark 6. Grease and flour a 1kg (2lb) loaf tin.

Place all the dry ingredients In a mixing bowl. Mix together well with a wooden spoon.

Add the water and combine to make a very soft mixture.

Place the mixture in the prepared loaf tin and bake in the oven for 30 minutes, or until the loaf sounds hollow when tapped on the base.

Turn out of the tin and allow to cool on a wire rack.

Tip: This bread is less moist than many traditional breads. Wrap the loaf in cling film once it is cooled to prevent it from drying out.

100   the gluten-free cookbook

desserts

fresh instant ice-cream

Enjoy the fruits of the season in this delicious cheat's ice-cream.

| prep time | serves 4 | 82 cals per serving | 2g fat per serving |

250g (8oz) frozen summer fruits, such as raspberries
1 banana or strawberry smoothie
1 small pot fromage frais

Place the frozen fruit in a blender or food processor with the smoothie and fromage frais.

Blend for a few seconds until smooth and serve straight away for a delicious soft-set ice-cream. For a firmer ice-cream, simply transfer to a freezerproof container and freeze for 1–2 hours before serving.

chilled lime soufflé

This prepare-in-advance dessert is sure to become a dinner party favourite.

| prep & cook time | serves 4 | per serving | per serving |

grated zest and juice of 5 limes
1 tablespoon powdered gelatine
3 large eggs
125g (4oz) caster sugar, plus 2 tablespoons for the egg whites
200ml (7fl oz) double cream, lightly whipped
25g (1oz) chopped pistachio nuts, to serve
grated lime or lemon zest, to serve

Put half of the lime juice into a small saucepan. Slowly sprinkle the gelatine over the lime juice, taking care that it is moistened and there are no dry patches. 'Sponge' (allow to stand) for 10 minutes.

Separate the eggs and put the egg whites to one side. Put the yolks, sugar, remaining lime juice and all the zest into a large glass bowl. Set the bowl over, not in, a saucepan of simmering water. Whisk the ingredients together until the mixture is thick and mousse-like and leaves a trail. Remove the bowl from the heat and continue to whisk until the bowl feels cool. Stir the whipped cream into the cool mousse mixture. Set aside for a few moments.

Put the saucepan containing the gelatine onto a low heat and let it gently dissolve, on no account allowing it to boil - try to avoid stirring. Cool for 1 minute and then stir into the mousse base.

Put some cold water and a handful of ice cubes into a large bowl. Sit the bowl containing the mousse and gelatine mixture in the iced water. Gently stir until the mixture thickens and begins to set. Remove from the ice.

Whisk the egg whites in a glass or metal bowl until they form soft peaks. Add the remaining 2 tablespoons of sugar and continue to whisk for a further 30 seconds. Fold the whites into the setting mousse mixture, taking care not to fold too much, or the mixture will be quite dense. Turn the mixture into a glass bowl or 15cm (6in) soufflé dish or into individual dishes, cover and refrigerate for 2 hours.

To serve, sprinkle the top of the soufflé with the chopped pistachio nuts and grated lime zest. Leave at room temperature for 15 minutes before serving.

Note: Pregnant women, babies, the elderly and those who are suffering illness should not eat raw or lightly cooked eggs. Use a pasteurised alternative.

fruity amaretti

A taste of summer you can enjoy every day.

20 mins		271 cals	9g fat
prep time	serves 4	per serving	per serving

125g (4oz) gluten-free Amaretti biscuits
250g (8oz) ricotta cheese
2 tablespoons fresh orange juice
2 teaspoons clear honey
250g (8oz) strawberries, halved
2 peaches, stoned and sliced

Lightly crush the Amaretti biscuits and place in the base of a serving dish or 4 individual dishes.

Place the ricotta cheese, orange juice and honey in a food processor or blender and blend until softened.

Alternatively, place the ingredients in a bowl and beat together well.

Scatter the strawberries over the Amaretti biscuits, then add a layer of peach slices and spoon over the cheese mixture.

Place in the refrigerator to chill. The biscuits will remain crisp for a couple of hours.

sweet crêpes

Now everyone can join in the traditional pancake toss.

prep & cook time   serves 4   56 cals per serving   2g fat per serving

125g (4oz) buckwheat flour
pinch salt
50g (2oz) caster sugar
2 eggs
250ml (8fl oz) milk
25g (1oz) butter, melted
lime or lemon wedges and caster sugar,
  to serve

Sift the dry ingredients into a bowl and make a well in the centre. Add the eggs and half the milk.

Gradually mix in the flour to make a smooth thick batter. Stir in the remaining milk and the melted butter. Beat for 2–3 minutes.

Leave to stand for 30 minutes before use.

Grease a heavy-based frying pan and place over a high heat. Pour in enough batter to cover the base thinly.

When the edges begin to turn golden, turn the pancake over and cook the other side. Keep warm, layering with greaseproof paper, whilst cooking the remaining pancakes.

Sprinkle with sugar and serve with lime or lemon wedges.

nutty marshmallow crunch

This nutty treat will appeal to the big kid in everyone.

prep & cook time | serves 6 | 295 cals per serving | 18g fat per serving

125g (4oz) good quality dark chocolate,
  broken into pieces
25g (1oz) unsalted butter
25g (1oz) unsalted peanuts
25g (1oz) raisins
50g (2oz) mini marshmallows
50g (2oz) white chocolate, broken into pieces
50g (2oz) flaked almonds, toasted

Put the plain chocolate and butter in a bowl over simmering water and melt. Stir in the peanuts, raisins and marshmallows until coated.

Turn out on greaseproof paper and wrap the paper around the mixture, pressing it into a 4cm (1½in) thick roll. Chill until firm.

Put the white chocolate in a bowl over simmering water and melt.

Unwrap the chilled roll, scatter the toasted almonds over a sheet of greaseproof paper and, working quickly, cover the roll in the melted white chocolate, then roll it in the flaked almonds. Wrap the roll up again in the greaseproof paper.

Chill until firm. Cut into thin slices to serve.

Note: Be sure to use gluten-free marshmallows and chocolate – some brands have added wheat products.

Variations
Add more fruity flavour by adding chopped up dates, apricots or other dried fruit.

For those with nut allergies, omit the peanuts, and roll in hundreds and thousands instead of flaked almonds. Check that the hundreds and thousands are gluten-free before using.

blackberry and apple pears

Quick to prepare and bursting with goodness, this fruit-filled dessert is the perfect end to a midweek supper.

prep & cook time · serves 4 · 106 cals per serving · 0g fat per serving

4 firm pears, cut in half lengthways and
  core removed
juice of 1 lemon
1 x 300g (10oz) can blackberries in natural
  juice
1 eating apple, cored and chopped
1 teaspoon ground cinnamon
300ml (10fl oz) unsweetened apple juice
1 tablespoon cornflour, blended with 2
  tablespoons cold water

Preheat the oven to 180°C/350°F/gas mark 4.

Sprinkle the pears with the lemon juice to prevent browning.

Drain the blackberries, reserving the juice. Carefully mix the blackberries with the chopped apple and cinnamon and 2 tablespoons of apple juice. Pile into the centre of each pear half.

Place the pear halves, stuffing side up, in a baking dish and pour over the reserved blackberry juice and remaining apple juice. Bake in the oven for 15–20 minutes until just softened.

Drain the pears, reserving the juice, and keep the pears warm. Mix the juice with the cornflour mixture and heat, stirring constantly, in a small saucepan over a moderate heat until thickened. Serve the pears with the thickened juice and yogurt or fromage frais.

Variation:
Replace the pears with apricots, either fresh or tinned in natural juice.

pistachio and almond milk pudding

Rice pud with a twist – down-to-earth noodles spiced up with a hint of luxurious saffron.

prep & cook time   serves 6   per serving   per serving

175g (6oz) unsalted shelled pistachio nuts
50g (2oz) blanched almonds
25g (1oz) fine rice noodles
50g (2oz) butter
600ml (1 pint) milk
5 tablespoons single cream
¹/₄ teaspoon powdered saffron
2¹/₂ tablespoons sugar

Place the pistachios in a bowl, cover with cold water and leave to soak overnight. Drain, and rub off the skins with a tea towel.

Put the pistachios and almonds in a blender or food processor and coarsely grind. Do not over grind.

Break the rice noodles into pieces about 10cm (4in) in length. Melt the butter in a large saucepan, add the noodles and cook, stirring, until the noodles are nicely browned, taking care not to burn them.

Add the milk and cream, and bring to the boil.

Reduce the heat, add the pistachio mixture, saffron and sugar, and simmer for about 15 minutes, stirring frequently. Serve hot or leave to cool.

chocolate and brandy dessert cake

A crunchy biscuit base and rich chocolately filling combine to create a deliciously luxurious dessert.

prep & cook time	serves 10-12	453 cals per serving	34g fat per serving

75g (3oz) gluten-free Amaretti biscuits, crushed
400g (13oz) plain chocolate, roughly chopped
4 tablespoons brandy
4 tablespoons liquid glucose
600ml (1 pint) double cream
1 teaspoon cocoa powder
icing sugar and Amaretti biscuits, to decorate

Grease and line a 23cm (9in) cake tin. Sprinkle the crushed biscuits over the base of the tin.

Put the chocolate, brandy and liquid glucose into a bowl and stand over a pan of simmering water. Remove from the heat when the chocolate has melted. Stir well and leave to cool.

Whip the cream lightly and stir into the chocolate mixture. (It is important that the chocolate mixture is not too hot.) Spoon the mixture into the tin, cover and chill for several hours or overnight.

To serve, run a palette knife around the edge of the dessert cake and turn out. Decorate with Amaretti biscuits and icing sugar and serve.

chocolate and cherry torte

Served warm or cold this indulgent dessert is perfect for rounding off a meal with friends.

prep & cook time | serves 8 | 391 cals per serving | 22g fat per serving

150g (5oz) gluten-free ratafia biscuits
2 tablespoons cocoa powder
50g (2oz) butter or margarine, melted

2 large eggs, beaten
100g (3½oz) caster sugar
100g (3½oz) rice flour
100g (3½oz) melted butter or margarine
1 teaspoon baking powder
3 tablespoons cocoa powder
3 tablespoons brandy
1 x 425g (14oz) tin black cherries
a few fresh cherries, optional

Preheat the oven to 180°C/350°F/gas mark 4. Lightly grease a 23cm (9in) spring-form cake tin.

Put the biscuits in a food processor and blend to a fine powder. Add the cocoa powder and pour in the melted margarine. Transfer this to the prepared cake tin, push the mixture in well and bake in the oven for about 10 minutes.

Place the eggs and sugar in a glass bowl over a saucepan of simmering water. Whisk until the mixture reaches blood temperature, then remove and transfer to a food mixer. Beat until the eggs have reached the ribbon stage. Pour the mixture into a large mixing bowl and, using a large metal spoon, gently fold in the flour and then pour in the melted butter or margarine.

Add the remaining ingredients and mix well. Pour into the cake tin onto the biscuit base and bake in the oven for another 35 minutes or until cooked.

Decorate with fresh cherries, if using, and serve warm or cold.

COOK'S TIP
Ribbon stage means that the eggs have thickened and turned a pale creamy colour. The mixture should be thick enough to fall from the beaters in thick streams or ribbons.

cranberry polenta cake

A deliciously fruity cake with crunch!

prep & cook time   serves 6   607 cals per serving   25g fat per serving

125g (4oz) polenta
250g (8oz) all-purpose gluten-free flour
1 heaped teaspoon baking powder
150g (5oz) golden caster sugar
grated zest of 1 orange
150g (5oz) unsalted butter
1 tablespoon orange juice
1 egg, beaten
1 tablespoon olive oil

For the filling:
250g (8oz) frozen cranberries
50g (2oz) demerara sugar
2 teaspoons polenta

Preheat the oven to 180°C/350°F/gas mark 4. Butter a 20cm (8in) loose-bottomed cake tin.

Place the polenta, flour, baking powder and caster sugar in a food processor with the orange zest, and process to combine.

Add the butter and process until the mixture resembles fine breadcrumbs. Combine the orange juice, egg and oil and, with the motor running, slowly pour into the processor through the feeder tube.

Once combined, stop the machine and press two thirds of the dough into the prepared tin.

Combine all the filling ingredients and pile onto the base, leaving a border of about 1cm (1/2in) around the edge.

Crumble over the remaining dough and cook in the oven for 45–50 minutes or until golden brown.

Serve warm with cream or crème fraîche.

index